"HUMOUR IN (AND AS) MEDICINE"

Dr. K.P. Misra is a renowned cardiologist and a brilliant teacher in the medical and other fields. He has about 100 publications, two books and audio-video cassettes on cardiology to his credit. He has received numerous awards and visiting professorships from many institutions and organisations. He has also received the Physician's Recognition Award from USA. He is a Fellow of the American College of Cardiology.

Dr. Misra is at present the Director, Medical Education and Senior Consultant Cardiologist at the Apollo Hospitals, Chennai. He is also the Director, Medical Services, ICI India Ltd.

HUMOUR IN
(AND AS)
MEDICINE

K. P. MISRA

Published by
Rupa Publications India Pvt. Ltd 1992
7/16, Ansari Road, Daryaganj
New Delhi 110002

Sales centres:

Allahabad Bengaluru Chennai
Hyderabad Jaipur Kathmandu
Kolkata Mumbai

ISBN: 978-81-716-7085-7

Nineteenth impression 2018

25 24 23 22 21 20 19

Typeset at Nikita Overseas Pvt. Ltd.

Printed at Nutech Print Services, New Delhi

THE AUTHOR'S ROYALTY ON THIS BOOK WILL BE DONATED TOWARDS LEPROSY ERADICATED PROJECT AT MADRAS SPONSORED BY THE ROTARY CLUB OF MADRAS, SILVER BEACH

Dedicated to my teachers and students
around the world
who have taught me in their own ways.
Life has been worthwhile
for their wonderful relationship.

PREFACE

I think life without humour is not only boring and monotonous but harmful for health. In the last two decades of my teaching and lecturing all over the world, I have found that the audience, whether they are doctors or lay people, always enjoy the jokes and humour in my lectures. It is universally true that humour adds spice and joy to lectures, whether technical or in any other field. I have been telling many jokes in my hundreds of lectures and they have all been appreciated by my students, colleagues and friends. I thought I would put many of these jokes in a book, which is the basis of this compilation. Though I have called the book *Humour in Medicine*, there are a few non-medical jokes, but the vast majority still pertain to the field of medicine and medical practice. Everyone knows that if one cannot laugh at oneself one cannot laugh with others. Thus, I have many times made fun of my own profession and my colleagues, which I hope will be taken in the right spirit by my professional colleagues.

Every country has one or two communities or ethnic groups to which most of the jokes are attributed. We have, for example, the Polish, the Irish, the Indians, who are responsible for the genesis of many of the jokes in the world. In today's world, where people cannot tolerate even jokes, I have deliberately avoided naming any particular community and therefore have only written the generic term of "a particular community" in some jokes.

This has an added advantage (besides not injuring the sentiments of those who mind the jokes) that every guilty-conscious community or their "enemies" will attribute the jokes appropriately to their advantage.

I hope everyone, including my doctor friends, students and colleagues, as well as people who are not involved in the medical profession, will enjoy these jokes. Many of these are my original jokes (from real-life experience or imaginative creations) but there are certainly some which I have borrowed from others from various sources over decades. I have forgotten the sources also over the years. I hope nobody will take me to court claiming to be the originator of some of these jokes. I believe there is no copyright claims over jokes in the world.

I am most grateful to Khushwant Singh, the witty and the most controversial journalist and writer of our country in the English language. I have been his great admirer (not necessarily of his ideas, but more of his wit and style of writing) for several decades and he has been very kind to go through the manuscript and even select a few of my jokes for his popular columns.

The entire secretarial work for this book was done by Indumathi Lakshman, who painstakingly and patiently tolerated all my eccentricities and repeated corrections to make the final outcome excellent by any standard. I must thank her for this. Lastly, I am most grateful to all my students and colleagues in the profession who have inspired me to write this book. I am also thankful to Subhash Sawant, Senior Creative Director and K. N. Subramaniam, Artist (Creative), HTA, who have kindly drawn the lovely and laughter-provoking cartoons for the book and also the cover page.

I wish all my readers Happy, Humorous Reading Times.

K.P.M.

If you are not allowed to laugh in heaven,
I don't want to go there. —Martin Luther

SUSA

1

There are lots of interesting medical definitions, for example:

A Neurotic builds castles in the air; a Psychotic goes and lives there; and the Psychiatrist collects the rent of that castle.

2

A Psychotic says: "2 plus 2 is 5". A Neurotic says: "2 plus 2 is 4 but I don't like it". The Psychiatrist, if asked what is 2 plus 2, says: "Pay my fees first and then we will discuss what is 2 plus 2".

3

A Physician knows everything but does nothing.
A Surgeon knows nothing but does everything.

A Pathologist knows everything and does everything but a little late (at postmortem).
A Psychiatrist knows nothing and does nothing.

4

Epitaph on a politician's grave: "Here lies the politician — as usual!"

5

Epitaph on a dentist's grave: "This is the last cavity he filled".

6

There are lots of interesting stories about the risk of surgery in a particular condition performed by the surgeon. There was one patient who was suffering from an advanced tumour and he went to a surgeon, who said, "I am sorry, I cannot operate on you, as the risk is 99%". The poor fellow went to another surgeon who also said the same thing. Very much disappointed and frustrated, he went to an eminent third surgeon who agreed to operate on him. The patient asked about the risk of surgery and the surgeon calmly replied, "It is about 99%". The patient-was shocked and said, "Sir, two other surgeons had refused to operate on me because they said the risk was 99%. How come you are willing to operate even with the same risk?" The surgeon smiled and replied, "Because I have already killed 99 and I was waiting only for you".

7

A medical thesis went to the USA for evaluation and the learned examiner, after going through the thesis, commented: "This thesis is good and original, but I am sorry to reject it as the good part is not original and the original part is not good".

8

I lecture quite a lot in different parts of the world. Once I was speaking in Muscat, Oman, and then invited some local people for dinner at my hotel. At the end of the dinner my local friend, who was not very fluent in English, said while proposing a vote of thanks to me and my wife: "We thank our hostess and host for their wonderful hostility".

9

At a psychiatrist's clinic a patient was seen

standing at the doorway when another patient came. The second patient asked the first one: “Are you going in or coming out?” The first patient promptly replied: “If I knew I would not be here”.

10

One of my alcoholic patients developed cirrhosis of liver, resulting in ascites. When I told him that his problem was ascites he asked: “What is ascites?” To make it simple I answered that it is accumulation of water in the belly, to which he responded in astonishment: “Where did the water come from? I always take it neat, never with water. . . . Oh, it must be that damn ice which I took with drinks”.

11

One of my alcoholic patients could not give up alcohol but was strict in taking only two pegs every day. After about 20 years of two pegs a day, one day he asked only for one peg. The barman asked in surprise: "Sir, I have been serving you two pegs every day. Why suddenly have you decided to take only one peg today?" The man replied: "My friend, I had taken a vow with one of my very close friends who is in Paris that we shall take one peg each for ourselves and one for each other". The barman asked with concern: "What happened today, Sir; did your friend die?" The man cooly replied while sipping his drink: "No, my friend, he is very much alive, but I have stopped drinking from today".

12

My popular statement in public lectures on how to stop smoking is: "It requires only will power not Wills power in the puff to stop smoking".

13

A certain minister was going by train and there were lots of people to see him off at the station. There was one man who, on being asked by the minister as to why he had come, said: "Only to pay my respects, Sir" . The train moved but the same man appeared at the next station and met the minister. Surprised, the minister asked: "Why have you come again, do you have some work with me?" to which the man replied, "No Sir, I have come only to pay my respects to you". This was repeated at the two subsequent stations and at last the minister got disgusted and asked in anger: "Why are you here again? Why don't you leave?" The man calmly replied: "Ok, Sir, now I have come to pay my last respects to you".

14

One of my old patients who had hysterectomy (removal of the uterus) said to her neighbour that they had removed her "hysterical rectum".

15

A patient was seen jumping up and down. On being asked what he was doing said: "I was asked to shake the bottle before taking the mixture but I forgot and that is why I am mixing it now".

16

The proverbial saying "familiarity breeds contempt" was always altered by my Professor of Gynaecology who used to say that "contempt" is superfluous and therefore it should be "familiarity breeds".

17

A girl student came running from her parents' bedroom and said: "Daddy, there is a female and a male fly in your bedroom". The father was very impressed and asked: "Are you so good in zoology? I am really happy". The girl replied that it had nothing to do with zoology. The father asked: "Then how did you know which one was the female and which one male?" The girl coolly replied "Very simple, Daddy, one was on the whisky bottle and the other on the dressing table mirror".

18

In one of my flights by Singapore Airlines the air hostess recognising me as an Indian asked, "Are you a vegetarian or normal?"

19

A person was seen going on the reverse gear around Connaught Circus again and again in a car and on being asked what he was doing said: "I am going to sell this car, so I am trying to reduce its mileage to get a good price".

20

A little girl in a school, when asked by the teacher if she knew the spelling of banana, replied: "Yes, Madam, but please tell me when to stop".

21

A boy was used to sucking his thumb all the time and his mother was very upset about it. On being advised by a friend, she told the boy: “If you keep sucking your thumb, your belly will swell up after some time”. After a few days a pregnant lady visited the house and the boy asked in innocence, “How long have you been sucking your thumb, aunty?”

22

Mrs. Indira Gandhi, while she was the Prime Minister, wanted to test the ability of some of the senior ministers in spoken English so that the one selected could be the President of the country. From the balcony of her bungalow she saw a young girl standing downstairs and said in Hindi, *Ek Kunwari Ladki Niche Khadi Hai*. Then she asked her ministers by turn to translate this statement into English as precisely as possible, to which one of the senior ministers promptly replied, "Misunderstanding". That senior minister became the President of India.

23

A senior minister of India was given a bungalow which was a lovely one near a railway station. He liked the bungalow but complained to Mr Nehru, the then Prime Minister, that the railway station would be a disturbance all the time. On being told by Nehru that he would get used to it after a month or so, the minister said, “Okay, Sir, I will then move into the bungalow after one month”.

24

Mark Twain, the famous American humourist, once said: “They say George Washington was great, because he could not tell a lie. But I am greater than him, because I can tell a lie but I don’t”.

25

Abraham Lincoln had not so cordial relations with his wife, who was too proud of her family, which was the famous Todd family. So, Lincoln used to say: “My wife’s family thinks so much about themselves that their family name is spelt with two d’s when even God is spelt with only one d”.

26

In my public lectures on hypertension I often say: "It is wrong to say essential hypertension (a term used for describing the common type of hypertension people suffer from) because it gives the wrong connotation that it is necessary to have a little high blood pressure". Then I add: "It is better to call it idiopathic (meaning no primary cause known) because idiopathic is that condition when the doctor is an idiot (not knowing the cause) and the patient's condition is pathetic".

27

One of my old patients came with pain in his right knee. After examining him I said: "You have osteo-arthritis in the right knee joint". He then asked me: "What is osteo-arthritis?" to which I replied: "It is a sort of old age problem of the knee joint". Then he asked me in right earnest:

"Then would you be kind enough, Doc, to tell the age of my left knee now?"

28

Once there was a search for Adam in heaven and a saint was asked to locate him quickly. The saint went around for a little while and brought Adam promptly. On being asked how he identified him, the saint replied: "It was very simple. He is the only one without a belly button".

29

The famous filmstar and humorist, the late I.S. Johar was once asked in his "Question Box" in the *Filmfare,* "When people get disgusted they say 'Go to Hell'; what do the people in Hell say?" Mr Johar replied: "They say, 'Go to India' ".

30

A critic of Mr. Johar's acting said: "You are such a lousy actor that you should not even try playing any role in films or dramas. Why don't you try your role as a female? Maybe you will succeed". Mr Johar promptly replied: "I did but the result was disastrous. I was playing the role of Sita in Ramayana on the stage and when Ravana saw me he ran away and refused to abduct me. So the drama ended with the audience throwing stones at me".

31

In the British Museum there was a small-sized skull and the new guide said it was the skull of a great prophet. On being asked, "How could it be when it is so small in size and the prophet had lived to old age". The guide promptly replied, "It is the skull of his childhood".

32

Physicians are known to be the talkers and surgeons the doers. Surgeons hate the physicians talking too much about various theories and hypotheses. On one occasion a gynaecologist, a physician, and a surgeon were to be executed for some criminal negligence in the hospital. The judge asked each one of them about their last wish before they were hanged. The gynaecologist said in response: "I would like to do five major operations before I am hanged". The physician said: "My Lord, I will be happy if you could kindly allow me to give a speech for one hour". The judge said: "That is very simple. We will certainly allow that". Then the surgeon, being asked about his last wish, hurriedly said: "My Lord, please hang me before this fellow opens his mouth".

33

There is a story about a man who was collecting brains of different specialists for study. A physician's brain cost only 5 dollars per pound whereas a gynaecologist's brain cost 10 dollars and a surgeon's 20 dollars per pound. On being asked why the surgeon's brain was so expensive the man replied: "You don't know how many surgeons you have to kill to get a pound of brain".

34

A famous eye specialist in Madras has his Nursing Home door designed in the shape of a human eye with all the details like pupil, iris, etc. A friend of mine visiting Madras and being shown this door commented: "Thank God, he is not a gynaecologist !"

35

I tell a lot of medical riddles in my lectures. One of them is like this: "A nurse and a doctor fell in love and got married. After a year they had a child, but the nurse said, "I am not the mother of the child" and the doctor said, "I am not the father of the child". What was the real situation? It is really very simple; the nurse was a male nurse and the doctor a lady.

36

One other riddle I tell in my medical lecture is: "Which is that milk that make men lower their pants and ladies raise their skirts?" People feel embarrassed about this riddle, but the answer is simple: "Milk of Magnesia" (which is a laxative given for constipation).

37

In China the most difficult operation is tonsillectomy, because nobody opens his mouth.

38

In my lectures on hypertension and obesity, I say, “Lifeline is inversely proportional to the waistline” (In Hindi: *Jitni Badi Kamar Utni Chhoti Umar*). I also say that most people are thin before marriage but when they get into middle age they acquire a little paunch and obesity. My friend then defined middle age as that age when the “middle portion” bulges out.

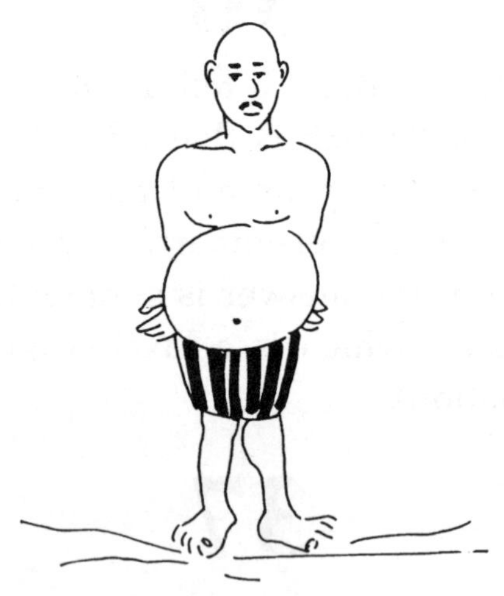

39

I always emphasise the usefulness and benefits of walking regularly in the treatment of high blood pressure and prevention of heart attack. Then I add that nowadays no one is walking regularly except one group of people. They are the opposition members in the assemblies and parliament!

40

On being told that the art of walking is lost nowadays my friend responded by saying: "Who says the art of walking is lost? How else do I go from my house to the garage?"

41

There are many examples of printer's devil in medical vocabulary causing havoc. A young lady patient of mine was operated in our hospital and the operation notes said: “After putting the patient on the operation table and application of antiseptics this young lady was raped (‘d’ got dropped from draped) in the usual manner”. On seeing this note and feeling very amused I went to our surgeon and asked him in innocence showing his notes: “Please tell me what is the usual manner?”

42

There is a heart drug called Inderal for the discovery of which Sir James Black got the Nobel Prize in Medicine. A pharmaceutical company claiming the benefit of Inderal said in their literature: “Inderal reduces morality”. The horrified publicity manager had to recall all the literature from all over the country because of this “reduction of morality”.

43

A person was found in a swimming pool late at night by the guard of a hotel. The guard shouted: "Don't you know that swimming is not permitted at this hour?" The man replied: "For heaven's sake I am not swimming. . . . I am drowning", to which the guard promptly responded: "Then it is OK".

44

An American was asked: "Do you talk to your wife while making love?" The American promptly replied: "Yes, if there is a telephone available nearby".

45

In Texas everything is supposed to be big. One visitor was given a huge hamburger to eat. When he expressed surprise at the size of the hamburger, he was told: "This is Texas. Don't you know everything is big here?" Then he was offered a huge bottle of beer and again when he remarked about the size of the bottle was told the same thing; "Don't you know, in Texas everything is big?" And the fellow got drunk and while going back fell into the swimming pool of the hotel. The guard saw him and on being approached by the guard the man said: "For heaven's sake, please don't flush!"

46

A mountaineer was looking for a suitable accommodation at the base of a hill but could not find any. After a long search he knocked at the door of a house and a lady came out. On being asked for the favour of accommodating him at night the lady said: "I am sorry. I am alone and I have only one bed, but if you don't mind we will keep a pillow between us and sleep on the same bed." The man agreed and spent the night. The next morning on being informed by the man that he was a mountaineer wishing to climb the hills, the lady said to the man: "Please go back without any attempt at mountaineering". The man asked in surprise: "Why not?"

The lady replied: "Because you could not climb even a pillow last night".

47

My most favourite sloka about doctors is *vaidyaraja namastuvyam yamaraja sahodara yamahniyati pranani twam prananicha dhananicha,* which in English means: "O, Doctor, I salute you as the brother of the Lord of Death (Yamaraja), but you are even worse because the Lord of Death takes only life, whereas you take both money and life".

48

One of my heart patients was travelling by train and was getting down at every station with his luggage, only to get into the compartment before the train started. On being asked about this peculiar behaviour by other passengers, my patient replied: "You will not understand, but I am a heart patient". The passengers were surprised with this statement and asked: "So what? Why are you getting down and again getting into the train at every station?" My patient replied: "Because my doctor has advised me not to take a long journey at a stretch".

49

My Chief in USA had a very interesting story to tell me about one of his old lady patients. There was this old lady who used to bring a big list of questions to ask every time she came for a check-up. My Chief was disgusted with the same type of questions being asked on every occasion, which wasted lot of his time. He quietly told his secretaries that if any of them could steal that list of questions from the patient's vanity bag, he would reward them with 10 dollars. At the next visit one of the secretaries sent the lady to the toilet on the excuse of collecting some urine samples and in the meantime stole the list from her vanity bag. She informed my

Chief about this and he was very happy. After examining the patient the Chief mischievously asked the old lady: "Don't you have some questions to ask?" The lady looked for the list of questions in the vanity bag repeatedly and on failing to find it in the bag said to the shock of my Chief: "I knew someday it would happen to me; that is why I have always kept a duplicate under my blouse", and then she brought the duplicate list out promptly.

50

A person of a particular community was travelling by train and he lost his purse in the toilet of the compartment and came out shouting that somebody should do something about getting back his purse which had a lot of money. On being asked why he didn't pull the chain, the man said "I did, but everytime only water came out".

51

I give a lot of lectures on controlling obesity which is a risk factor for high blood pressure and heart attack. On being asked how to reduce obesity, I said, “Please understand that obesity is like your savings account. How do you reduce your savings account? By either depositing less in your account or spending more from your

account. The same way to reduce obesity depositing less means eating less and spending more means doing exercise to use the accumulated fat". I was very happy with this apt analogy which impressed a lot of people, but one fat banker got up and said: "Doc, you don't understand my problem. I don't have a savings account. I have only a fixed deposit". I was absolutely stunned and could not find words in response.

52

On being told that two pegs of alcohol may not do harm, one of my chronic alcoholic friends said: "You don't understand my problem. I take only two pegs on every occasion". I just laughed and said: "I have seen you getting drunk with many pegs on every occasion in parties and you want me to believe your story?" to which he replied: "You don't understand. I take only two pegs . . . but after that I am not I".

53

There is a lovely Birbal story about the solution to the eternal question "Chicken first or egg first?" It is believed that a man once came to challenge Birbal, the witty minister of Akbar, with questions. Birbal was in a great hurry but on being forced by Akbar to take the challenge of the stranger he said to the challenger: "I am in great hurry. Please decide whether you want to ask one most difficult question or a hundred easy questions. I will surely reply as you wish". The man was very happy and said: "I shall ask only one but a most difficult question." Birbal said: "Please go ahead". The man immediately asked: "Chicken first or egg first?" to which without batting an eyelid Birbal replied: "Chicken first". The challenger promptly asked: "How do you know?" Birbal smiled and said: "You can't ask that because you decided to ask only one question to which I have replied".

54

In a Church the priest was giving sermons, saying: "God created the world. He created animals, plants, and us, the human beings". There was a scientist's son in the audience who immediately got up and said: "Father, why do you say so? My father is a scientist and he has a different viewpoint". The priest asked: "What is his view?" The boy replied: "My father says, we came from monkeys", to which the priest responded by saying, "That is OK, because we are not talking about your family but the rest of us".

55

One of my friends defined Block Development Officers (BDOs) as the ones who block development. They have indeed succeeded in their objective!

56

My Professor of Radiology used to teach about studying the breast shadows in the X-rays saying: “They come in three sizes; the ping pong, the ding dong, and the king kong”.

57

One little girl was asked if she knew what a particular machine was (being shown a weighing machine). The girl replied: “I don’t know what this machine is about, but everytime mummy stands on this machine, she just screams”.

58

Medically, it is a well-known fact that a smile requires only four muscles whereas frowning requires sixteen. Then why frown?

59

A little girl in the school was asked to give an example of how heat expands and cold contracts. She replied: "Simple, Sir, the days are longer in summer and shorter in winter".

60

One of my American friends visited Andhra Pradesh, where very hot-chilli food is served. Without knowing, the American friend took a handful of chilli powder served on rice, appropriately called by Andhra people "gun powder", and started jumping and crying with tears rolling down his cheeks. I was shocked and asked my Andhra friend to help him. My Andhra friend said to the American: "Please take some icecream and you will be all right". The American took icecream and became quiet. But next morning he was heard shouting from his hotel toilet: "I want icecream now". My Andhra friend was helpless and informed him that there was no icecream suppository; only oral preparations were available in the market.

61

Going by train through West Bengal towards Howrah station and watching hundreds of people on both sides of the train defecating in the open between the train and their houses, my doctor friend commented: "I have seen houses with attached toilets but here every house is attached to a toilet".

62

The famous doctor Lippes who invented the loop for family planning had an interesting slogan which was put up at every meeting he addressed: "Loop before you leap".

63

One of my not-so-educated patients who was married for a long time but did not have a child complained about his wife to me: "Doc, my problem is my wife is inconceivable No, no, I mean she is impregnable. No, no, I am sorry, she is actually unbearable".

64

There was a signboard prominently displayed at a shop which was shown to me when I asked for a discount: "Discount given to everyone above 75 years if accompanied by both parents".

65

I have put a little notice in my chamber which says: "Everyone brings joy to this room — some when they come and some when they go".

66

My Professor in USA used to put up a slide before his lectures which said:
"For a House Physician — 90% work and 10% talk
For a Registrar — 60% work and 40% talk
For an Associate Professor — 40% work and 60% talk
For a Professor — 10% work and 90% talk
And in that capacity I am here to talk".

67

My secretary was taking a dictation from me when two other colleagues arrived and started discussing the matter being dictated, and in fact started contributing to the dictation by me. My secretary threw up her hands and said: "I cannot manage three dictators at a time when people hate even one dictator".

68

Everybody knows about the efficiency of Indian Telephones. Once a businessman was demanding a payment on trunk call from the customer, when the customer started pretending his inability to hear. The businessman started shouting louder but the customer kept saying that he was not able to hear. At last, the operator who was listening to the conversation intervened and said to the customer: "What do you mean you cannot hear. I can hear very clearly", to which the customer responded by saying to the operator: "If you can hear, then you pay. Don't interfere in our conversation".

69

When I was working in the USA there was the annual competition to decide the best teacher by the Residents of our hospital. One of my Residents informed me that he had voted for one particular doctor who was considered the dumbest among all staff. When I expressed surprise at his choice the Resident replied: “Well, he is the best teacher as I have learnt the most from him”. When I asked “how?”, he said in reply: “Everytime he opens his mouth and teaches I go to the library immediately to check if he is right and that is how I have learnt the most from him”.

70

Once there was a seminar on pericardial (the outer covering of the heart) diseases. The Chairman, Dr Noble Fowler, said in his introductory remarks: “I don’t know why I have been called to chair this session, because I am merely a cardiologist and not a pericardiologist!"

71

One of my patients when advised against smoking and drinking, used to say: "All good things of life are either illegal, immoral, expensive, or bad for health"!

72

A person entered the Emergency room of a hospital with a small girl and on being

questioned whether they were related to each other answered: "Yes, but distantly". The doctor asked him: "How distant?". The person replied: "Quite a bit; we are fourteen brothers and sisters; I am the eldest and she is the youngest!"

73

A person could not succeed in any method of family planning and had ten children. The doctor speaking to him was very annoyed and asked him: "Why don't you ask your wife to use a contraceptive?" to which the man replied: "I did that and these two children came after that (pointing to two of the ten children)". The doctor then said: "Why don't you use some condoms?" to which the man replied: "I did that Sir, and these two came after that". The doctor was shocked at the failure of the methods mentioned and then said: "Why don't you get vasectomised?". The man replied very sorrowfully: "I did that Sir, and these three came after that". The

SUSA

doctor was absolutely shocked at the failure of vasectomy also and said in anger: "In that case why don't you keep away from your wife and live separately for two/three years?" to which the man replied in innocence: "These three came after that, Sir".

74

A new PG student joined the department of Psychiatry and wanted to read a book on care of the child. One of the mischievous Senior Residents suggested to him a book titled "Unwanted Child" by F L Burst! The new Resident went on searching for the book in the library and could not locate the book much to the amusement of the lady librarian and the Senior Residents.

75

When I worked in the Department of Gynaecology I was very happy and smiling and the nurse asked me the reason for being so happy, to which I replied: "When I worked in the Medicine Department I used to imagine myself suffering from medical diseases like tuberculosis, etc. . . . Similarly when I worked in the Surgery Department I used to imagine myself suffering from surgical diseases like peptic ulcer, appendicitis, etc. . . . But this is the only Department where I cannot suffer from any disease and that is why I am happy".

76

An obese patient came to my clinic and on being advised to take simple diet asked me: "Doc, please tell me what is the diet and whether I should take it before or after meals".

77

One of the difficult things for medical students is learning to express themselves in correct English. We had a Professor of

Ophthalmology who was very particular about the correct use of English. Once a lady student asked him: "Sir, I want to check my eyes". The Professor corrected her and said: "You mean to say you want your eyes checked?" The girl didn't understand and said again: "Sir, I want to check my eyes". The Professor got annoyed and asked: "Why do you want your eyes checked?" The girl became nervous and replied: "Sir, I don't look well", to which the Professor responded by saying: "I am sorry, then I cannot help. It is God who gave you that look".

78

There used to be a Minister of Law and Company Affairs who visited Hyderabad. An old unmarried man called on the Minister and said: "Sir, I am an old, lonely bachelor and I believe you are the Minister of Company Affairs. Please help me, Sir, by arranging some company for me as well as some affairs!"

79

At the Niagara Falls from the Canadian side there is a tunnel taking tourists behind the Falls. My wife and I, with a group of tourists with a large number of ladies, went inside the tunnel and reached the spot behind the Roaring Falls. Our guide said: "If the ladies stop talking for a moment, you can hear the roar of the Niagara Falls".

80

There used to be a story about the after-dinner speech. Once a lion in a circus got out of the cage and became violent and started attacking people. The ringmaster could not control it and appealed to people if any one could volunteer to control the lion. Two of the spectators jumped into the ring one after the other and were eaten up by the angry and violent lion. The ringmaster got desperate and again appealed for someone to control the lion. One brave young man jumped into the arena and quickly whispered something into the lion's ear, after which the lion tamely got back into the cage. Much to the relief of everyone the ringmaster closed the cage but asked the young man in astonishment: "What did you do to the lion to make him so tame?" The young man replied: "It was very simple. I just told the lion: "You may eat me, but you have to give an after-dinner speech".

81

One of my medical students came to me for help in his love affairs and said: "Sir, I am in trouble. Can you please help me". I asked: "What is your problem?" He replied: "Sir, I am in love with a girl and have made 50% progress. You have to kindly help me now". I asked: "What do you mean by 50% progress?" He then replied "Sir, I am in love with her but she is not responding".

82

They recommend *Sirsasan* (the head stand in yoga practice) for improving blood flow to the brain. My Professor used to say: "That depends on how much is empty up there! If there is emptiness, only then blood can flow and fill up the vacuum".

83

Doctors and lawyers are known for their

greed for money and professional fees. It so happened that a doctor and a lawyer were sitting next to each other at a dinner party when an emergency call came for the doctor. The doctor was upset and did not want to be disturbed and said to the lawyer: "I don't think I should be disturbed here. Don't you think so?" The lawyer coolly replied: "I think yours is a noble profession and you should attend to such emergencies". The doctor reluctantly left the party to attend the call. Next morning the first thing the doctor saw on his table at his clinic was a bill from the lawyer for his "timely advice".

84

Chitragupta (the Minister of Yamaraja, the Lord of Death), once got a patient who arrived in heaven. He checked the list and did not find the patient's name and said: "How did you come here when your time has not come?" The man said. "I don't know. I was sent here". Again within a short time half-a-dozen people arrived without their names appearing on the list of Chitragupta who asked in despair: "What is happening here? How the hell are you all coming here without your names appearing on my list." On deeper enquiry Chitragupta then found out the reason. All the people mentioned a particular doctor's name in that area and then Chitragupta exclaimed: "Oh, that explains. That doctor is known to send people here earlier than expected!"

85

One of my Indian friends in the USA visited his home in south India with his children who were born and brought up in the USA. On their return I asked my friend's son: "What is the thing that impressed you most in your south India trip?" The boy had never seen people wearing dhoti in the USA and therefore said to me: "Uncle, I was really surprised to find that even adults in India wear napkins!"

86

There goes the story of giving the child the vocation of his aptitude by an aptitude test. A rich man used of offer each of his children on a plate a stethoscope, a hammer, a pen and paper, which a maid brought. Each child used to be then given the training for preparing him to become a doctor, an engineer or a writer according to his choice of the article on the plate. Then came the child who had to undergo the same test. The maid brought all the articles on the plate and the child was asked to select any one of the items. The child selected the maid and rejected the other items much to the shock of the parents.

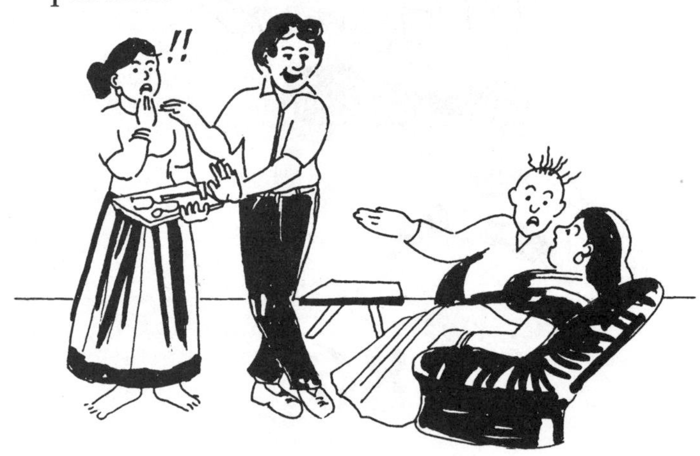

87

I once made a call to Bombay on STD and each time got the same wrong number. Ultimately the man in Bombay said to me: "I am sorry, Sir, you are getting in my number again and again. Why don't you tell me the Bombay number and I will ask your friend to call you back". I was very grateful to such a benevolent person and gave him my friend's number. After waiting in vain for half an hour, I dialled again and got another wrong number. The man was very angry to be disturbed and said to me: "Why do you disturb me? This is not the number. What do you want?" I coolly replied: "I want my original wrong number because he was more helpful than you are", and put the telephone down.

88

Once a Sikh, a Hindu, a Muslim, and a Christian priest met and were discussing their collections from offerings from devotees after conducting worship and prayers. The Christian priest said: "I throw all the collections into the air after drawing a cross on the floor and whatever falls on the cross goes to the Church and I take the balance for myself". The Muslim priest said: "I also follow a similar principle. I throw all the money after drawing a crescent on the ground and whatever falls on the crescent goes to the mosque and the balance to me". Similarly the Hindu priest also said he followed a similar approach after writing OM on the ground. Then all of them looked at the Sikh priest who said: "I am deeply religious. I cannot think of taking anything that is really not due to me. So, I throw all the money up into the air and whatever God takes is His, and the balance that falls on the ground I take in all humility".

89

Once a premature baby was born to a couple on the seventh month of pregnancy and on being asked to suggest a name for the baby the doctor replied: "Why don't you call him a 'Rocket' because he covered the distance of ten months in seven".

90

A French lady was learning English and after a month or so wanted to thank the lady who had taught her English. The French lady said: "I am sorry to have cockroached on your hospitality". The English lady corrected the French lady saying: "You mean encroached", to which the French lady replied "I am sorry, I had forgotten that I am addressing a lady".

91

The people in my state are so lazy that

they don't want to really work for anyone or for anything. Once it so happened that a boat was stuck on the seashore when the tides had gone low and the water had receded from the beach. Hundreds of my people tied a rope to the boat and were pulling it to bring it into the water. Everyone seemed to be doing his best to pull the rope and the boat was not moving. Ultimately, the rope broke (it was a weak one) but much to my amazement no one fell down. Such is the hard work of my people.

92

Our librarian in the USA used to tell me a lovely story about a person being investigated for a long time in a USA hospital to establish the cause of his jaundice. Ultimately all the tests were found to be normal, when a smart physician detected the cause. The patient was a Chinese.

93

My Professor used to ask us: "Why are the eyes of the Chinese not slanted?" When we could not answer satisfactorily he used to say: "Because they are constipated and they strain a lot in the toilet".

94

The Chinese philosopher Confucius used to say: "A busy road does not grow grass and a busy head does not grow hair!" (Confucius himself was a bald man.)

95

One Company made lot of profits and offered a foreign trip to all their senior managers along with their wives. The trip went off very well and everyone seemed to have enjoyed it. The Managing Director wrote a personal letter to each of the wives thanking them for their co-operation and asking them if they enjoyed the trip. Almost all the wives replied asking the Managing Director: "Which trip?"

96

One lady was found fanning the wet grave of her late husband. The people visiting her were very touched by her gesture and said: "You are so attached to your husband that even after his death you want to give him some comfort?" The lady replied: "It is not that; I had promised my husband that I will not marry anyone until the grave is dry".

97

Sri Ramakrishna Paramahansa used to tell a story about the futility of acquiring knowledge that is not applicable in life. Once a learned pandit was crossing the river in a boat and the ferryman was illiterate and quite ignorant. Both being alone in the boat, the pandit asked: "Do you know the Vedas and Upanishads?" to which the ferryman replied: "Sir, I am ignorant of these things as I am illiterate". The pandit responded by saying: "Then half of your life is lost". Then after some time the pandit asked again: "You may not know the Vedas and Upanishads but you must know the Ramayana and the Mahabharata", to which the ferryman again replied: "I am sorry, Sir, I do not know these as I am illiterate". The pandit was very upset and said: "My friend, three-forth of your life is lost". Then, after sometime, dark clouds appeared on the sky and winds started blowing hard and the boat started tossing in the midst of high waves in the

river and the ferryman asked the pandit: "Sir, do you know swimming?" The pandit sorrowfully and in fear replied: "No", to which the ferryman promptly responded by saying: "Your whole life is wasted now, Sir, whereas my life will be saved".

98

At the hospital twin babies were delivered but the mother was surprised to see one baby fair-complexioned and the other dark. She asked the doctor the reason for this and the doctor replied: "Madam, the fair one is the original and the other the carbon copy".

99

There was one Khadak Singh who was such a terror that people used to say *Khadak Singh khada honese khidkiyan khadakte the.* The poor Khadak Singh got married and after six months people started saying *khidkiyan khadaknese Khadak Singh khada ho jata hai.*

100

Once Mahatma Gandhi was asked: "What do you think of civilization in Europe?" to which the Mahatma replied: "It is a good idea".

101

In a village there was a massive family planning campaign and almost every eligible man was vasectomised by the aggressive doctors. Then one unmarried young man volunteered to be vasectomised and the doctors in surprise asked: "Why do you want to get vasectomised when you are not married?" The young man promptly replied: "I know that, but when everyone is vasectomised in the village but something goes wrong and a pregnancy occurs they will all blame me".

102

On an application form the candidate was asked to give his name, age, sex, etc. He filled in the form and wrote his name and age and then under 'sex' wrote "occasionally".

103

One of my patients, who was a pilot, used to get checked by his official doctor in Bangalore who always advised him against smoking and drinking. The pilot was very disgusted with this official doctor and used to complain to me about this doctor's impractical advice. After a few months I met the same pilot at a party and he appeared to be very happy. I asked him: “Why are you so happy today?” to which he coolly replied: “That damn doctor who never smoked and drank died today”.

104

Once we were being taken on a tour at Atlantic City, USA. The guide was very nice and was explaining to us the various places of attraction. One of the most attractive places was, in fact, a cemetery full of flowers and gardens. The guide said: “This is a beautiful cemetery but unfortunately people living within 5 km of this cemetery cannot be buried here.” We were all surprised and asked: “Why not?” to which the guide replied: “Because they are living”.

105

Two children entered a gallery of modern art and were alone watching the paintings they could not understand. After some time they said to each other: "Let us run away from here, lest they blame us for all this".

106

When two psychiatrists meet, one asks the other: "You seem to be OK. What about me?"

107

My Professor, who was a physician, used to say that surgeons and dacoits are similar, because both wear masks and both carry knives to do their jobs.

108

One of our friends got a telegram that his mother-in-law was dead. He was asked whether she should be buried or cremated. He promptly replied: "Do both Why take chances?"

109

The wife asked her husband: "Darling, last year you had presented a lovely chair to my mother on her birthday. What are you going to give her this year?". The husband coolly replied: "We will electrify it this year".

110

There was a Hakim with a scoundrel and fraud as his assistant. After working for a few years with the Hakim, the assistant ran away with some tablets, tonics, etc. and opened a new clinic of his own at another village and appointed a new assistant for himself. The first patient came suffering from diarrhoea and the fraud prescribed a few pills to be taken by the patient. The patient and the attendants went away, but next day in the morning a larger number of villagers were seen approaching the clinic with lathis and stones. The fraud got worried and asked the people: "What happened? Is the patient all right?" The villagers replied: "The patient is dead but that is not the problem. He is still purging. Who will take him to the cremation ground? Both of you better come and take him to the cremation ground." The fraud and his new assistant had to agree and did take the patient to the cremation ground with the Chief on the head side and the poor Assistant on the leg side. They felt relieved after the cremation and came back. Next day the villagers came with a case of constipation. The fraud deliberated over the problem and asked his assistant to give some black pills for the patient. The assistant looked hesitant but on being asked again to give the pills said: “I do not care about the colour and size of the pills but the head side must be mine this time”.

111

A little girl from the Protestant Church and another small boy from the Catholic community were playing on the beach, both naked. A boy approaching both of them and on learning that they were Christians of different denominations, exclaimed after looking at both of them critically: “Oh God, there is so much of difference between a Catholic and a Protestant!”

112

An old lady called a plumber to repair her bathroom and after a few minutes the plumber came out and gave his bill for 50 dollars. The lady was shocked and said: “Oh God, how can you charge 50 dollars for such a small job. Even my doctor doesn't charge this much". The plumber coolly replied "I know that, because I used to be one".

113

Interestingly both adulteration and adultery come from 'adults'. Children never do these things.

114

There used to be a modern artist who was very famous for his paintings. Once an exhibition was being held and the organisers approached him for the contribution of an item. The painter obliged, and after a few days left the painting in his house to be collected by the organisers, as he was going away on tour. His little children not knowing the worth of the painting soiled it with their excreta much to the horror of his wife. The wife felt very sad but kept the painting in one corner of a room in the house. Unfortunately the organisers came to the house when the wife was also away and the children innocently handed over the painting to the organisers. After a few days the artist came back and the wife was too horrified to tell him anything. In sheer ignorance the artist went to see the exhibition which happened to be the final day of the exhibition. He saw a big crowd and heard his name being announced as the winner of the first prize by the learned judges sitting on the dais. Much pleased with this, he stood there looking at the reaction of people when he heard the chief judge explaining the reason for which he got the first prize. The judge said "This painting has been awarded the first prize because it is so natural that it smells!"

115

When I was in the USA in the late 60s the first computer-written poems were published, on which the *New York Times* wrote an editorial which ended saying: "The poems are excellent and certainly a breakthrough. Of course, the computer doesn't understand what it writes. But so what? Neither do the modern poets!"

116

There was an obstinate atheist who never believed in God. On his deathbed however he called some priests to convert him to religion and acceptance of God. The priests were surprised and asked him why he wanted to do it when all his life he had objected to believing in God. The atheist replied: "Please convert me into believing in God and make me a theist so that after death I will feel happy that another theist had died".

117

On the grave of a very lazy person the epitaph written was: "He was so lazy that he stopped breathing one day".

118

One psychiatrist was told by his patient: "Doc, my problem is I have double vision every time. Every article I see is two." The psychiatrist asked: "Can you know which is real and which is fake?" The patient replied: "No". Then the psychiatrist said: "That is good. I will remember you very well when you make payment for my bill twice".

119

I met one of my friends after a very long time and while chatting did complain about the little family quarrels between husband and wife. My friend said: "We had the same problem, but soon after our marriage we decided not to fight and promised that one of us would go out of the house if there was any occasion for fight." I was very impressed and asked him if this was successful. He said: "Of course it was successful. Can't you see that I am so healthy because I am leading mostly an outdoor life now".

120

Statistics, they say, is like a bikini — it reveals a lot but hides the vital parts.

121

A statistician is one who will tell you that if a man is standing with one foot on a hot oven and the other on a slab of ice, on the average, the man should be comfortable.

122

A mother was trying to impress on her daughter the value of getting up early by saying: "Look darling, it is the early bird that catches the worm", to which the little girl responded: "Then what about the early worm which got caught?"

123

I attended a seminar on allergy and the chairman said in his opening remarks: "Anything under the sun as well as the sun can give allergy." Some consolation for allergy patients!

124

Amebiasis is so common in our country and so protean in its manifestations that my professor used to say "Amebiasis in India can mimic any condition except pregnancy!"

125

In the Mount Sinai Hospital in the USA where I worked, I had a problem every time my Chief came on rounds, because he would ask me about the various bio-chemical parameters of the seriously ill patients in the Intensive Care Unit. He knew very well that every day and every time we did correct the bio-chemical imbalance which was a routine procedure for any Resident like me. I began getting annoyed about this being asked every day. So I complained to the Deputy Chief quietly, "Why should he ask me these things every day when he knows fully well that we do correct any imbalance immediately?" My Deputy Chief assured me that he would take care of this next day. The next day again on rounds when the Chief asked me about the bio-chemical parameters of one of my very seriously ill patients, the Deputy Chief immediately intervened and said to my chief: "Don't worry about that problem because our patients die in perfect bio-chemical balance".

126

My Professor used to say that patients die either with an "O" sign or a "Q" sign — "O" meaning the mouth being open like the letter "O" and "Q" meaning the tongue protruding out at the corner of open mouth.

127

Being asked what medicine is used when the patient is almost dying, the new Resident replied, "Aqua Gangetica Five drops" (meaning a few drops of Ganges water).

128

If showing teeth is smiling, then the tusker always smiles.

129

A beautiful lady was in a two-piece swimming suit when the manager in charge of the swimming pool complained: "Madam don't you know that two-piece swimming suits are not allowed here?" The lady replied: "Then tell me which one of these pieces I should take off?"

130

My friend used to say that sarees are like

medical text books — they have to be bought when a new edition comes, whether you use it or not. (His wife was very fond of buying sarees of new designs.)

131

One of my patients continued to point to his tummy whenever I started talking to him. He was not responding at all to any of my questions. I was getting annoyed when the patient's attendant appeared and explained to me that I must talk with my mouth at his tummy level because the patient has swallowed his hearing aid.

132

I was visiting a Wild Life Sanctuary with my friends from England. When the evening came we wanted to stay there and approached a lodge for accommodation. The receptionist was very co-operative. I asked him if rooms were available, to which he said: "Yes, rooms are available". Then I asked if meals were available. He again replied: "Yes, meals are available". I asked if transport was available to take us the next morning. He politely replied: "Yes, transport is available". Then I asked: "What about mosquitoes?" He smiled and replied: "They are also available".

133

A gentleman asked a stranger on the roadside if he had change for a 100 rupee note. The stranger replied: "No, but anyway, thank you". The gentleman asked him surprised: "why 'thank you'?" to which the stranger replied: "For the fact that you considered me a possessor of 100 rupees".

134

When two deaf persons met on the roadside the conversation went like this: "Are you going to see a movie?"
"No, no, I am going to see a movie."
"Oh, I am sorry I thought you are going to see a movie."

135

A person from a particular community arranged a house-warming party in his own house. The guests, while enjoying the party, suddenly discovered that the house didn't have a ceiling. On being asked about this, the person replied: "Don't think I am a fool to waste money on this. Haven't you heard that the government has decided to put a ceiling on all urban property?"

136

One very good thing about my wife's cooking is that it is not habit-forming!

137

Once a sadhu died, and when he went to the abode of heaven and hell he was taken to both the places to decide about his choice. The lady in charge of hell showed the sadhu a beautiful area with gardens and flowers and the most beautiful ladies working around with attractive dresses and very enjoyable music being played all over the place, etc. Then he was taken to the heaven side and was shown a very gloomy picture of serious people with closed eyes, and not talking to each other. The sadhu was asked to make his choice between hell and heaven. The sadhu decided for hell thinking all his life he had done so much penance that he deserved the enjoyment that was in hell. So he was taken to the hell and again saw the same beautiful atmosphere. He was enjoying every bit of hell when after a short while he was asked to escort the lady to another area of hell which was really frightening because people were being thrown into burning fires and boiling oil pools, etc. The sadhu was stunned and asked the lady: "what the hell is this? I thought you showed me the hell on the other side which was so beautiful and enchanting and that is how I selected the place." The lady coolly replied: "That is correct, Sir, but that was only our Marketing Department."

138

Once President Bush, Mr Gorbachev and Rajiv Gandhi met God and one after another they asked about their country's future. First President Bush asked: "Oh God, when is my country going to be the best and the greatest in the world?" God replied: "It will take about 50 years", and President Bush started crying saying: "Oh God, I shall not be able to live to see that". Then came the turn of Gorbachev who asked the same question, to which God replied: "It may take about 100 years". President Gorbachev started crying, saying: "Oh, I shall never be able to live to see that happening". Then came the turn of Rajiv Gandhi who also asked the same question. There was a long pause, after which the God started crying.

139

There was a policeman at the police station,

who was corrupt and charging Rs 500 for even registering an FIR from any person. A person who was honest saw the photograph of Mahatma Gandhi with his right hand raised with the open palm in a blessing hanging behind the policeman. The person berated the policeman: "How can you be so corrupt as to ask Rs 500 when you have the Mahatma's photograph on your back?" The policeman calmly replied: "That is exactly why I am asking only for Rs 500", pointing out at the open hand of Mahatma Gandhi and saying: "The Mahatma says that the minimum is 5".

140

Once Bernard Shaw was in a party with a very talkative man sitting next to him and continuously boasting about his knowledge in all subjects under the sun. Mr Shaw tolerated this for a while and then said to the gentleman: "You know something? Between the two of us we know everything in the world". The man appeared to be very pleased and asked: "How is that Mr Shaw?" Shaw coolly replied "You seem to know everything in the world except one thing which I know That completes the entire field of knowledge." The man asked: "What is the thing I do not know which you know?" Shaw replied: "The fact that you are a big bore!"

141

Once a teacher and a politician met and the politician asked about the teacher's job and salary. On being asked why he was continuing as a teacher when the salary was so low, the teacher replied that it was a noble profession and his father as well as his grandfather were also teachers. The politician then said: "So what if your father and grandfather were teachers? Suppose your father was a rogue and grandfather a scoundrel, then do you think you should also become a rogue or scoundrel?" The teacher calmly replied: "No, then I will become a politician."

142

Once Mr Rajiv Gandhi and two of his friends were stranded at Lakshwadeep on a small island surrounded by sea with a lot of sharks. They did not know how to get out of the island when his businessman friend ventured into the sea and was quickly devoured by the sharks. There was again a long wait but no rescue team being available, the filmstar friend also jumped into the sea in desperation, but was again quickly swallowed by the sharks. After again a long wait Mr Gandhi could not wait further and jumped into the sea and swam across with the sharks approaching him but immediately returning without doing any harm to him. On reaching a safe place, the people who were astonished about his escape from the sharks asked Mr Gandhi how did he manage this. Mr Gandhi said, "I didn't do anything except telling all of them that I had nothing to do with the Bofors money". Now the people understood that even the sharks did not swallow it.

143

There was a Scotsman carrying a bottle of whisky in the back pocket of his trouser. He fell down and broke his hip and then felt some fluid dribbling on the back of his thigh when he said: "I hope it is blood!"

144

There is a politician who is Chief Minister

of a state. In an emotional speech in a public meeting he said: "I love my country so much and I am such a great patriot that I have given up my life so many times for my country!"

145

Mark Twain was a heavy smoker. He used to say: "I don't know why they say giving up smoking is difficult? I have given it up so many times".

146

Mark Twain also spoke about some of the strict rules he followed in his smoking habit. "I have some principles to control my smoking. I never smoke two cigarettes burning at a time. . . I never smoke while asleep, and never refrain while awake."

147

There was a seminar on the life span of

stars and planets. One learned speaker said that sun was the source of all life and its life span was 1 billion years. On hearing this statement an old lady in the front row appeared very worried and asked the learned speaker: “Did you say 1 million years or 1 billion years?” The speaker replied: “1 billion years”. The lady said with relief: “Thank God, I thought you said 1 million years.”

148

I used to have a classmate who was not good at his studies at all. In our second year in Medical College we had a question in the Physiology paper asking us to write on “water balance” (this is about how the body maintains the balance of water in daily activity) with illustration. My friend did not know a word about “water balance” and kept looking at me for guidelines as I was next to him in the examination hall. I could not help him because it was too long a subject to be given in hints and gestures. Ultimately as the exam came to an end he drew a lovely picture of a Rajasthani lady with a number of pots containing water balanced on her head.

149

Once J Krishnamurthi, the famous philosopher, was asked if he was the reincarnation of Lord Buddha which Rajneesh had claimed. Krishnamurthy asked, "How does he know?" The person who asked the question couldn't say anything but after some hesitation asked again: "What do you think of Rajneesh?" to which Krishnamurthy promptly replied: "I don't think of Rajneesh".

150

On one occasion a flight was coming from Belfast to London when one of the four engines of the plane failed. The pilot came on the microphone and announced this and said: "There is nothing to worry as the other three engines are working: but we may be delayed by 15 minutes or so." Then after sometime the second engine failed and again the Pilot announced: "I am sorry that the second engine has failed, which is a big surprise: we will be able to manage with the other two engines, but maybe we will be delayed by another 15 minutes or so." After some time surprisingly the third engine also failed and the Pilot announced: "I don't know what is happening. I can't even believe it, but please do not worry as we will be able to land with the only engine left, but there may be a further delay by a few minutes". The plane ultimately landed safely and a number of journalists approached the passengers to know their reactions and feelings about this unusual event. One Irish passenger was coming out when he was asked: "Suppose the fourth engine had also failed, what do you think would have happened?" The Irish promptly replied: "Oh God, then we would have been in the sky for a much longer time!"